The Lord Mount Dragon

Keith Ruttle

Illustrated by
Rowan Barnes-Murphy

CAMBRIDGE
UNIVERSITY PRESS

One day, a poor weaver got up early to make some porridge for his breakfast.
He started to work while the porridge cooled, but he soon fell asleep.

It was a hot summer morning and, when the weaver
awoke, his porridge was covered with black flies.

3

The weaver was angry. He raised his hand and slapped it down
onto the flies. Then he looked down. All the flies were dead!
He counted them out carefully. There were seventy.

The weaver felt very pleased with himself. He went outside
and said to his neighbour, "I killed seventy with one blow!"
His neighbour didn't believe him. He just laughed.

The weaver was angry again. He said to his neighbour, "If I can kill seventy with one blow, I ought to be a noble knight, not a poor weaver. I will leave today to seek my fortune."

Then he realised that a noble knight must have a suit of
armour. So he went back into his kitchen to see what he could
find. He found some saucepans, a small three-legged iron pot
and a large cooking pot with a big, heavy lid.

He made a suit of armour by sewing the saucepan lids onto his tunic and apron. Then he put the three-legged iron pot onto his head to make a helmet. The pot had a hole in it, but he didn't mind. "It will help me to keep a cool head during my battles," he thought.

Then he picked up the big, heavy pot lid to use as his shield,
and painted a sign on it. The sign said: 'I am the noble knight
who killed seventy with one blow.'

The weaver marched outside in his new armour. The saucepan lids clattered loudly as he walked, but it didn't bother him. "The noise will make my enemies run away during my battles," he thought.

He climbed onto his donkey (he was not rich enough to own a horse) and set off to seek his fortune. His neighbours laughed and shouted, but the weaver could not hear them because the iron pot was covering his ears.

The weaver decided to go straight to the king and become his champion. "After all, I am the noble knight who has killed seventy with one blow," he thought proudly.

All along the road to the castle, people came out to see him.
The weaver thought that they were cheering and waving. Actually,
they were laughing and pointing.

At last, the weaver arrived at the king's castle. The king had heard that he was coming and was very amused.

The king sent a soldier to greet the weaver at the castle gate. "His Majesty welcomes the noble knight who has killed seventy with one blow," said the soldier grandly.

The weaver felt very proud indeed. Surely he would make his fortune now.

In fact, the king was planning to play a cruel trick on the weaver.

A dragon was roaming the land and eating people. The king had already sent many brave knights to kill the dragon, but they had all failed. Most of them had been fried by the dragon's fiery breath and eaten up in one great gulp – horses, armour and everything!

"I do have a job for you," said the king. "It should be easy for a noble knight who has killed seventy with one blow."

Then the king told the weaver about the dragon. He said that the dragon lived in a dangerous swamp and had already eaten many brave knights.

The king gave the weaver a horse and a small bag of coins and sent him off to kill the dragon. He didn't expect to see him ever again.

The weaver didn't really want to meet a dragon who liked to eat brave knights. He thought that he might just take the bag of coins and ride straight back home instead.

However, the king had thought of this. The horse had been trained to gallop straight to the dragon's swamp without stopping. The weaver could not slow it down or turn it around, however hard he tried.

He rode on and on for three whole days. Then, at last, he arrived at the dragon's swamp.

As the weaver approached, the dragon rose slowly
from the swamp. It was huge and ugly.

The weaver jumped down from the horse and climbed quickly up a tall tree. He was not a moment too soon, because the dragon pounced upon the horse and ate it up in a single gulp! Luckily, the dragon could not reach the weaver or else it would have eaten him, too.

Soon the dragon fell asleep, right underneath the tree where the weaver was hiding. The weaver heard it snoring and started to climb down the tree as quietly as he could.

Suddenly, a branch broke and he fell down – right on top
of the dragon!

The dragon woke up and tried to shake the weaver off,
but the weaver clung on tightly to the dragon's ear.

The dragon was furious. It roared into
the sky, fire blazing from its nostrils.

The dragon was so angry that it forgot to look where
it was going. It flew straight towards the king's castle, crashed
into the castle wall (CRUNCH!) and fell to the ground, stunned.

The king had seen the weaver riding the fiery dragon across the sky.
He was amazed. He ran down to the courtyard, where the dragon now lay.

The weaver was proudly standing over it. "I decided to bring the
dragon back for Your Majesty to kill," he said.

The king quickly took a sword and chopped off the dragon's head.

Everyone cheered.

"Since you are already a noble knight, I will make you
a lord instead," said the king.

Then the king named the weaver 'Lord Mount Dragon', in honour
of his fiery ride across the sky. He also gave him one-fifth of the
kingdom, which happened to include the weaver's own village.

So it was that, the very next day, the weaver and the king rode together into the weaver's village at the head of a magnificent procession.

The weaver was wearing brilliant new silver armour, which he
thought suited him very well. He was carrying the biggest and
most colourful banner in the whole parade. The banner said:

I am the Noble
Lord Mount Dragon
who rode a fiery Dragon
and killed seventy
with one blow